Peter Jacoby

Unlocking Your Creative Power

ISBN 1-883368-00-6

RAMSEY PRESS
11586 CESPED DRIVE
SAN DIEGO, CALIFORNIA 92124

Manufactured in the United States of America

Second Printing

March 1993
San Diego, California

Contents

Preface

"The Workshop"
— or —
"Whither this book?"

It was 1987 and John West went "Gulp!". It was a "gulp" that could be heard in three counties (one of them, San Bernardino, is the largest county in the lower 48 United States—*data point*). At the time, John was the Director of Arts & Humanities for the University of California, Irvine, Extension, and I had just proposed the Workshop (or: *The Workshop*) to him. And he had said "OK." Well, it was really more like: "OK? (Gulp!)"

〜〜〜

I had just finished teaching a 10-week course in advertising copywriting for the Extension. In the course of the course (of course) I made a profound discovery: I was attempting to teach Applied Creativity to a roomful of people who had very little grasp of Creativity—their *own* Creativity—or how to get in touch with it. I recognized a need, and proposed to John how to fill it.

As I see it, the difference between Creativity and Applied Creativity is this: Creativity is (and is the ability to have) ideas—to conjure, to think where no one has thought before, to give mental and emotional birth and recognize the idea thus born, to put the Tinker Toys® and Lincoln Logs® together in new ways no one else had ever done before, or to find a new use for the ways they had been put together before. It's the ability to see pictures *before* they are painted, words before they are written or spoken. And it's the ability to make up new words.

Applied Creativity is taking Creativity and applying it to a specific goal, such as, well, such as "concepting" (that's an advertising word) and writing an ad for my advertising copywriting class.

Most of the folks in the class were struggling with trying to apply to a goal something they'd lost touch with, or were afraid they

8

didn't have at all. I looked around me outside the copywriting class, and thought about so many people I had known over so many years. I realized that it wasn't just the class. Most people I have come in contact with have lost touch with the extent of their creative power. And, knowingly or not, each of them mourns the loss.

(I want to make a very important point here about this book, and it is this: This book is focused on *unlocking* your creativity, NOT on *applying* that creativity toward solutions to specific situations. The world already abounds with excellent books dealing with the application of creativity. Or, if it doesn't abound, at least there are a lot of them. *This* book follows a simple, fundamental, and, therefore, often overlooked principle: First things first.

(Perhaps my next book will be applications focused. Perhaps not. In the meantime, this book is intended to assist folks with getting back in touch with a very powerful part of themselves which has been, to one degree or another, repressed or, at least, neglected.

(This focus on *unlocking* your innate creativity—as opposed to *using* your creativity to design a better widget or fix better lunches for the kids—in no way lessens the power or validity of the book. In fact, I think it enhances it. Too many folks become too frustrated too often by being shown how to—or asked to—perform more creatively when they really, deep in their hearts, don't feel they *are* creative.)

So I decided to put together a three-day weekend workshop designed specifically to get people not only back in touch with their creative power, but also to make them comfortable with it. All I had to do was figure out how.

I went to my basic assumptions: 1) *Everybody* is born creative; and 2) I am fundamentally the same as everyone else on the planet.

I looked back over the more than three decades of my career —all but two weeks of which have been in what most would agree were squarely in the Creative Arena: Theatre (as an actor, a designer, a director), music (musician, producer), writing (poetry, screenplays, magazine articles, short stories, "thank you" notes), photography (including one magazine cover), painting (yes, I've even sold a few), television (writer, director, producer), film (writer, director, editor), and advertising (writer, director, creative director, marketing strategist).

Then I asked myself: What worked—and *still* works—for me? What has allowed me to continue to believe I'm creative enough to be able to accept that many creative challenges and successfully apply that much creativity over so many years? That's when it hit me. It wasn't other peoples' "tricks" or "techniques" for sparking *moments* of creativity at all. It was simple, fundamental truths. And, I firmly believe, they are simple, fundamental truths for everybody, not just for me. So I sniffed and poked and otherwise investigated these simple, fundamental truths until I was pretty sure I knew how they worked.

Also, I was certain that the best way to impart an understanding of these truths to other people would be for them not so much to hear about them as to *experience* them—to experience *themselves*— just as I had in my investigations of them, and in my life. "Experience is the best teacher"—that's a fundamental truth. Also, they are so often the *experiences* of the vagaries of life which cause people to move away from their creative power—that, too, is a fundamental truth.

From there, I loosely borrowed, or modified, or made up (from scratch, so to speak) exercises and other devices I thought would enable people to get back in touch with—to experience—something they started with and had only lost touch with, not lost: their own individual creative power.

And *voilà*, the "Unlocking Your Creative Power" ™ © Workshop was born. To my great joy, it has thrived since. In fact, it has thrived to the extent that I have written this book not out of vanity or lack of good movies to watch, but out of demand. And out of a sincere desire to speak to far more people than will even go through the Workshop.

So here's the book.

But it is here with a couple of slight (very slight) apologies. To those who have taken the Workshop, please bear with the repetitions of what you've already been through. For you, my intent for this book was to give more explanation, more philosophical meat to many of the exercises and other devices you experienced in the Workshop. To those who have not taken the Workshop, it was my intention that this book be as *experiential* as reading a book can be. I fear reading about it can never be quite the same as experiencing it (it's sorta like sex in that way). But it can be close. Very close. So, both of you, please know this: I think I hit a pretty happy medium and I believe this book will have great value for each of you.

One other thing I discovered in putting together the Workshop, and then "running" it, is another fundamental (and two-part) truth: 1) One cannot *teach* creativity; 2) happily, one doesn't have to —all one has to do is *unlock* it.

Thank you, John West, and Laura Ferejohn (John's assistant) for taking the chance on the Workshop in the first place. Thank you, everyone who has gone through the Workshop, for coming and playing with me. And thank you, Geni (my wife), for being content to go to bed with the foot warmer (our Holstein cat) instead of me the many nights I stayed up late to get this book written.

And now, to all: Enjoy!

Peter Jacoby

Unlocking Your Creative Power

Chapter 1

"I'm not creative," and other myths.

If you haven't actually said "I'm not creative," you've heard it. Either from someone else, or from inside yourself. Or you've run across: "What I do isn't creative." And there are so many other variations on this theme:

- "I wish I were more creative."

- "I don't know how to be creative."

- "I'd like to do something more creative, but I don't know how and I don't think I can."

"I wish I had a more creative job, because it would be more fun."

"I don't mind not being creative. Someone has to tend to all the practical stuff."

Et cetera, et cetera, et cetera . . .

It's not a fun feeling. In fact, it can be a very desperate feeling. If some of these sound familiar—and they most likely do or you wouldn't have bought or borrowed this book—don't spend too much time feeling exclusive in your despair. We all, at one time or another, wish that we both *were more creative* and *lived our lives more creatively*. Not to mention exercising more creativity on the job.

That's the bad news. Few of us are exercising the level of creativity we would like. Few are living up to our creative potential. But in that last statement is a hint of the good news. The good news is this:

We all have a potential for creativity which, in almost every case, far exceeds our creative achievement to date. Interestingly, what we have done over the years is "walk away from" or even "*run away from*" that potential. We've also "given it away" by the pound, and even constructed quite elaborate means to deny that it exists. Why? Because it scares us. It threatens us. Or at least a part of each of us. But what an important part. It threatens who and what we have spent a lifetime becoming, and it threatens a major portion of the value system we have spent that same lifetime adapting to and adopting. Unbridled creativity threatens our adulthood, and our membership in good standing in the world of other adults.

That's scary.

So we deny it, block it, refuse it, turn from it, and use any number of other rather creative means (interesting, huh?) to keep our adult world and its many values intact. It has never ceased to amaze me, over the years I have conducted the Workshop, to witness just how much creative effort—and just plain effort, for that matter—is put into *not being as creative as possible*. All the while lamenting the lack of creativity, and expressing the desire for it.

It would seem that we are actually more creative than we want to be, and we're doing everything in our power to stifle that creativity.

In all fairness, perhaps a better way to put it is that we are more creative than we are *comfortable* being.

There is, of course, a rather perverse—and pervasive—logic to all this. It fits in with a whole universe of contradictory logic that we have had to deal with all our lives—and even have come to embrace. Let me try out just a very few examples of this logic on you, and see if you don't recognize it every now and then.

- Money is not the true measure of a person's value in this world; *I should be making more money than he or she does because I contribute more to the bottom line than he or she does.*

- Beauty is only skin deep, and is no measure of who or what a person is; *I've never seen a homecoming queen who looked like a pickle.*

- Laugh, and the world laughs with you; *did you see that wacko down on the corner laughing for no reason?*

• The only truly meaningful acceptance of you by others is unconditional acceptance of who and what you really are; *dress codes*.

There's a lot of contradictory stuff we face every day, and—surprisingly—a lot of it we accept, even though it feels unnatural or uncomfortable. That's an especially important point. We don't feel natural or comfortable when we find ourselves smack dab in the middle of a contradiction. Which is, in large measure, why we don't feel comfortable with creativity—the concept of it, or *being* it. Because creativity is contradictory.

I'll get back to this contradiction in a bit. But first, a little exercise to begin to better understand and be more comfortable with creativity.

With a pencil, copy this pattern of dots at least three times onto any convenient piece of paper or other surface. (But a surface you are willing to mark up. Coffee tables, floors and outside walls of homes are not recommended. Not prohibited—just not recommended.) In the Workshops this exercise is done on chalkboards. Or whiteboards. Or newsprint . . . Whatever.

This exercise is very much like games you most likely played as a child. The instructions are simple:

For each nine-dot pattern you have made: **Connect the dots.**

After you have connected the dots, rejoin me on page 24. But do go ahead and page 23. I'll wait.

Please don't look ahead in the book. That's cheating. More to the point, it's cheating YOU. Not me, certainly. I've done the exercise already. So have many others in the Workshop. They didn't cheat because they couldn't. I was there and this book was not. The point, though, is that if you choose to cheat, you only cheat yourself. I recommend against it, because if you do you'll have done nothing but waste your time and the money you spent on this book. The rest of the book will be based on the assumption that you won't cheat. It makes your life better and mine simpler. Thank you.

I'm willing to go out on a limb and bet your dots are connected something like this:

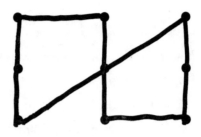

Or like this:

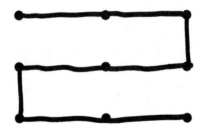

Or even this:

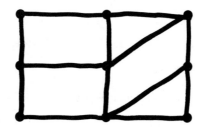

If so, you are like 98+% of the people who have done this exercise in the Workshop. During the exercise several rather interesting things take place. See if some of them were true for you.

I always ask for volunteers to "connect the dots," but then almost always have to *assign* volunteers to the task. I believe this is for several reasons, chief among them being:

- People want to see what others are going to do in order to judge whether what they themselves have already visualized they would do is "right" or "more clever" or "as smart as" compared to the others. Perhaps the strongest of these is the desire to discover if what they would have done was "right" or "correct."

- People are afraid to take a risk in front of other people, especially when what I like to call the "Rules of Engagement" are so loosely defined (i.e., "connect the dots").

- Knowing that nothing in life is that simple, they want to know what the "trick" is before they do the exercise—once again, so they can be "right."

Another interesting dynamic is that after they have been "volunteered" they study the dot pattern—sometimes for quite some time. There's a trick in there somewhere, darn it all. This is an important dynamic. Through the years we have learned that we can be one of two things: Right or Wrong. The goal of life is to be right more times than the other guy. Failure is being wrong. Connecting the dots is usually seen as a puzzle with one right answer and any number of wrong answers. People will often sit staring at the dots, agonizing over what the one right answer might be. Sometimes seemingly forever. After learning for so long and in so many ways the importance of being "right" (often learning the hard way), anything else is just about unthinkable.

(If there is a "trick" to this exercise, it is simply this: There is no *one* correct dot-connection pattern. *Any and all* patterns are correct, as long as the dots have been connected. In other words, you can't be wrong.)

Once the exercise has been done by enough people to fill several chalkboards (or whatever . . .), I ask everyone to look at each one of the dot-connection patterns and identify the similarities. In an ardent search for the "right" answer, most identify similar line patterns, or go even farther afield and note "mirror-image" line patterns. Before long, someone will note that all the line patterns are on chalkboards. Someone else will then comment that they are all in the same room. While these wags get a laugh or two from the others in the room, they don't realize they are getting warmer, closer to identifying some significant similarities. And closer to realizing more of their creative power.

Two glaring similarities always strike me right away. The first and most important is that almost without exception everyone stays within the "implied border" of the dot pattern:

~~~~~

27

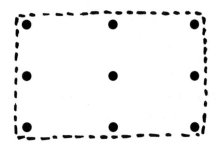

Very seldom does anyone go outside this border. But that's understandable. Can you remember, as a child, coloring in your coloring book, having a whale of a good time until some adult came along and suggested—lovingly, caringly, sternly . . . whatever—that you should *stay within the lines*? Have you ever said it to a child? It's OK to answer yes to either of these questions. It's what happens. It's a very normal part of growing up and beginning to learn what adult expectations are, what is expected of you if you are to be accepted as an adult later on in life.

In fact, "staying within the lines" is, many times, an important and necessary thing to learn. It's what keeps driving relatively safe for you and the others on the road. It's what keeps lining up for theatre tickets or checking out at the grocery store or anything from being a frustrating, maddening mess. It's what encourages you to cross the street at crosswalks and, by convention, decrease your chances of becoming a pedestrian fatality.

Staying inside the lines has another, more emotional benefit. When we don't know the answer or the correct procedure, it is one of the better ways to assure, as much as possible, that we will be "right". Or, at least, it's not our fault if we're "wrong." And if we have learned anything, especially in twelve or more years of schooling, being right is very externally rewarding. And being wrong is, often, brutally punishing.

The price we all pay for these benefits and many more like them, of course, is learning that self-expression and going outside convention into the unknown—unbridled creativity—is *not* a desired course of action, or at least is loaded with risks.

Another similarity in the dot connections is that, for much the same reasons as staying within the implied boundary, the lines connecting the dots are usually straight—or fairly straight. Neat. Controlled and contained. Something else we learned along the way from those experts around us: Adults.

There is yet another strong similarity which is so obvious—so obvious, so simple, and so "untricky"—that usually no one sees it. As I said, in the Workshop this exercise is done on chalkboards, and I put the dots on the boards with a piece of chalk. (I instructed you to make the dots with a pencil.) If you've guessed it already, good for you. But you still can't skip ahead.

Everyone connects the dots using chalk.

In your case I'm willing to bet you used the same pencil you drew the dots with. Why? No one—neither you, nor anyone in the Workshop—is told to use the chalk (pencil) to connect the dots. In fact, I make a point of putting the chalk back in the chalk tray before I say to each person doing the exercise, "Connect the dots."

Why chalk (pencil)? Implied rules. They're like implied borders. *Implied-rule logic* is something like: "He used the chalk to make the dots; he didn't say to use anything else; using anything else is 'going outside the lines,' which I have learned is discouraged, if not unacceptable; if I take the initiative to use anything else, I will be wrong and thought less of, or at least thought of negatively; not rocking the boat is *safe*."

Of course, most of this process is unconscious, but hard at work nonetheless. For a very good reason: It's something we've been taught, we've learned, and we've believed for a long, long time. And it is one more layer of repression capping our creativity.

This is not to say that chalk (pencil) shouldn't be used. It's just to point out that the more creative approach is to at least *entertain the possibility* of using something else. *At least ask the question* without fearing the answer.

How did you do? Did you agonize, even just a teeny bit, over discovering the "right" solution? Did you stay within the implied boundaries? Did you connect the dots using straight lines? Did you use the same pencil you used to make the dots in the first place? If your answers to these questions are "Yes," take heart. You are a normal late-twentieth century North American with lots of company. Read on. If you answered "No" to all of them, you don't need this book. Go forth and be more creative in all you do.

Having discovered some of the things we've learned over the years, and continue to use to lock up our creativity, let's have another

go at it. As before, create three sets of nine-dot patters using a
pencil to make the dots. And, as before:

For each nine-dot pattern you have made: **Connect the dots.**

Don't turn to page 34 'til you're done. I'll wait.

Notice anything different about the ways in which you connected the dots this time?

It's quiz time. In relation to this exercise so far, answer these questions (and, by the way, keep your completed dot-connection exercises for the next chapter):

1. In what ways were your dot-connection patterns different the second time than the first?

2. Why?

3. In what ways did you *feel different* when you connected the dots the second time compared to the first?

4. Why?

If your dot-connection patterns (and methods?) were different the second time, congratulations on your enhanced awareness of your own creativity, and your willingness to use it. Contrary to what you may have believed before, you *are* creative.

Chapter 2

"Where do ideas come from?"

Take a look at the second set of dot-connections you created. Not a good, hard look. More like an easy, resting look. In a sense, just point your eyes at them. Your creative power will do the rest. So let it.

If you are like most people, one of the (usually) informal games you played as a child—and may still play as an adult, with any luck—was sitting or lying back in a lawn chair or in the soft grass and looking up at the clouds. You let your mind go, let it wander wherever it would. Soon, you began to see things other than clouds. Castles. Horses. Monsters. Mountains. Heroes and villains. Men and women. People and things. Bits and pieces, such as a smile, or the head of a fish, or the prow of a boat, or a hand raised in salute or threat. Subtle shadings gave your imaginings even more detail—and truth. The monsters moved. The horse turned.

The boat became a truck or a rhinoceros or the biggest shock of wheat south of Montana.

How? They were only clouds. How?

Take a look at your dot-connections. Do the same thing you used to do with clouds. Do you begin to see things in the patterns made by connecting the dots? An ear? A dog? A sailboat? A campfire?

How? They are only dots and (probably, but not necessarily) lines of some sort. How?

Millennia ago, people sat outside at night and looked up at the stars. They connected *those* rather fancy dots and came up with some pretty fantastic images. Rams and crabs and balance scales and archers and a warrior wearing sword and scabbard, just to mention a few. Take a look at a map of the constellations and you may think that some of those "figures" are pretty fanciful, at best. But there they are. And there they have been for thousands of years. First in other, early peoples' imaginations, now in ours.

How? They are only stars? ("Only stars!" Isn't it amazing that, knowing what an amazing energy machine a star is, we can say things like, "*Only* stars?" But I digress . . .)

Before we get to an answer to that, let's try another exercise. Let's connect the dots again, but this time, instead of nine dots, let's try 25—five dots by five dots. Draw that out a few times and "connect the dots." I'll wait.

I always find it interesting how, once people have begun to look at "connecting the dots" in a new perspective, such as we did in the first chapter, each time they connect them it becomes more fun, and much freer. That's a very important clue about creativity.

Now take a look at your new, larger dot-connections. How many different things can you see in each one? More than in the nine-dot patterns? Of course. Because you have more to work with. Bigger clouds, so to speak. Write down some of the things you see. Then show the dot-connections to someone else and ask them if they can see anything in them. Do they see the same things as you? Can you see the same things they see?

Do they know what on Earth you're talking about? Chances are, if they haven't been doing this exercise, they will be more hard put to see anything at all. That's a measure of how far you've come in getting back in touch with your creative power in a very short time.

I like to call each of the dots "data points." Data points are what your head—mostly your subconscious—is full of. They are colors and smells and feelings. They are emotions—hurt and love and pleasure and caring. They are experiences—your first kiss, and your best one; the last time someone got really angry at you; just about all the times you've been really scared; the smell of Thanksgiving, and Christmas trees, and July 4th fireworks; the music that makes you cry; the taste of your tears; the way you can hear Niagara Falls through your feet. They are everything you've ever seen, heard, smelled, felt and tasted. And everything you've ever thought, good and bad.

If you don't think those data points are there, just pause for a second and remember the first time you were ever pulled over by the police for a traffic violation. You can still taste the fear. Yes, all those data points are there. Most of them are yours exclusively. Some you share with others—you can mention being at Woodstock to your friend who was also there and immediately you will both experience many of the same data points.

As you can well imagine, there are countless data points in each of us. "Billions and billions," as Carl Sagan might say. But what do they have to do with creativity?

Everything. They are the foundation and raw materials of our creativity. They are, indeed, the stuff dreams are made of, and dreams are, arguably, the ultimate creative effort. The difference between how they work and how we *let* them work is what causes so many of us to feel uneasy about our creative abilities. And how we feel about our creative abilities is, in large measure, what determines how creative we let ourselves think we are. And let ourselves be.

How did you see castles in clouds? And how did people first see constellations in the night sky? How did you see a sailboat or whatever in your dot-connections? The same way you get ideas, the same way you create. When you did the dot-connection exercises, you connected the same pattern of dots in three or more separate ways. Looking at the patterns, your mind literally raced through countless dot (data point) connections until it recognized something, associated what you were seeing with something you had seen (or imagined) before. You found a *similar* pattern. A boat. A tree. A dog. Your mind connected countless dots and evaluated the pattern to see if it was in any way useful. If it wasn't, the pattern was thrown aside and a new pattern was made. If a pattern was created that seemed in some way appropriate, it was hung on the "possible use wall," and then new patterns were made. Your mind went through heaven knows how many patterns—patterns made by instantly connecting and reconnecting billions and billions of "dots"—editing out the patterns that didn't relate until one familiar pattern stood out from the rest as the most appropriate: Castle. Then it was fine-tuned to fit the "external" pattern (dot-connection, cloud, whatever . . .) and, *voilà*, you saw that particular castle. Simple.

Simple, but not easy. Not yet anyway. But the good news is that it's simple. In fact, it's intuitive. You do it all the time, often without even realizing it. To unlock more of your creative power, what you want to do is *realize* it more. Make it more of a cognitive process as well as an intuitive one. Not instead of—*as well as*. In other words, you want to take a more active, conscious role in the process. And I don't blame you, because it's a lot of fun. To make it simple *and* easy, a few more parts of the process have to be understood. Like the difference between *Cosmos* and *Chaos*.

These two words are handy Greek antonyms which, between them, account for, well, probably everything. *Cosmos* is a Greek word for order. *Chaos* means a lack of order. To better understand what they have to do with you and creativity, it's back to paper (or whatever) and pencil (or whatever). Make a chart that looks something like the one at the top of the next page. (Neatness doesn't particularly count here. What counts is that you can read and use it. So make it something you can both write on and carry around. Not the wall.)

Cosmos	**Chaos**

Now start filling in the chart with words for things, actions, conditions, states of mind and/or body, etc., in the column for which you feel they are most appropriate. Such as:

Cosmos	**Chaos**
Order	Disorder
Structure	Random

What other words can you think of to put in one column or the other? (By the way, there doesn't always have to be an antonym for any particular word you chose for either column.) Where would you put "Risk?" How about "Safe?" And "Messy?" "Logical?" "Irrational?" "Rules?" "Expectations?" Where would you put "Game?" How about "Play?" "Fun?" "Work?" "Answers" and "Questions?" "Control" and "Letting Go?" Where would you put "Child" and "Adult?" "Creativity?" Don't just think about it. Write it down on your chart. When you're done, turn the page and take a look at how I'd divide up these examples.

Cosmos	Chaos
Order	Disorder
Structure	Random
Safe	Risky
Logical	Messy
Rules	Irrational
Expectations	Play
Game	Fun
Answers	Questions
Work	Letting Go
Control	Child
Adult	Creativity

Does mine look anything like yours? Are there any surprises? I suspect there may be one or two, or we wouldn't be the individuals we are. But I would also suspect that the two lists—yours and mine —are substantially similar. So what do these lists—yours and mine —tell us?

In a nutshell, that as we set aside "Childlike" things and took on the "responsibilities of Adulthood" and, of course, all of our well-learned lessons concerning Adult Expectations and Adult behavior, we allowed ourselves to set aside many of our "Childlike"—*chaotic*—priorities.

I remember times in my Childhood when I was willing to Risk life and limb without a second thought in the pursuit of Fun and new experiences. I'm sure you can, too. Which raises the question about two more concepts: on which side(s) of the *Cosmos/Chaos* list would you put "Status Quo" and "New & Unknown?" For me, Status Quo is *Cosmos* and New & Unknown is *Chaos*. And I'm willing to bet that's true for you, too. Status Quo is Safe. We know our way around there. We don't know what to Expect in New & Unknown. We can —or believe we can—exercise a comfortable degree of Control in Status Quo. Untrue in New & Unknown. Status Quo offers us reasonable, achievable Expectations of ourselves and others. Not so with New & Unknown.

So, for the most part, as reasonable, responsible Adults we favor the Status Quo. (Interestingly, to a very young Child practically

⌢⌢⌢

45

everything is New & Unknown.) Then, as we learn about bits and pieces of this huge New & Unknownness and make it into our Status Quo, we look for more New & Unknown. It's the Child in us which is nearly always willing to scamper off into the New & Unknown, just for the *Fun* of it.

But, as I said, the more Adultness we take on, the more of that willingness to explore the New & Unknown we put away, opting instead for the reasonability and predictability of the Status Quo. Put simply, as Adults, we don't like Chaos. We prefer Answers over Questions. We want everyone to follow the Rules, and we feel that simple Play—as opposed to tightly Structured Games—are somehow beneath our Adultness.

What's happening here is simple. The more of a stake we have in our Adult world, and the more we feel we have to lose if we don't exercise tight Control over that world, the more we do, consciously and unconsciously, to protect it. We set the Status Quo in cement, then use sunlamps to dry it all the more quickly.

One particular form of protection we learned—mostly in school in the course of twelve or more years—is to move out of the Question and to the *One Right Answer* as rapidly and in as straight a line as possible. Over the years, we've been pretty soundly conditioned to embrace this principle.

You don't believe me? Try this.

The pop quiz for this chapter is a very short and simple bit of word association. I'm about to give you a word. As soon as you read it, notice what feelings it conjures up for you. Ready?

Test.

How does that word—and, really, the meaning behind the word—make you feel? Can you remember how you dreaded finals? How did you feel about being called upon in class to Answer a Question or provide an explanation? Do you remember all the strategies you used to avoid being the one to be asked to get up before the class and explain the *Moby Dick* allegory, the past perfect tense, X-Y coordinates, where Albania was on the map, or the social impact of quantum physics? They were all tests, and they're all data points which are still alive and quite well, thank you, in your brain.

And I'm willing to bet none of those data points is especially comfortable.

This is not strictly a school phenomenon, either. How about the tests you had to take to get your driver's license—especially the driving test? And at work, how about a performance review, or having to explain your department's P&L situation at the staff meeting? How about asking someone you like for a date? Or remembering your spouse's most special wants and needs?

They are all tests. And we don't like them. Why? Because with every test we take, we run the Risk of being wrong. Of failing.

And we end up being afraid of Questions. We want Answers. More than that, we want *right* Answers. So we won't fail. So we can be right. So we won't lose.

What's so important about that? If there's anything in the world we've learned and taken completely to heart, it's that being right and winning make us Safe. Yes, we have come to believe that in a world of uncertainty, Safety is possible. All we have to do is follow the Rules, meet the Expectations, maintain the Status Quo, and we will be Safe. So will all that we have become, all we have accumulated, all that gives us identity and status, all we have spent our lifetimes building.

As long as we shun the New & Unknown, mitigate Risk, and have—or be able to create quickly—all the right Answers, the world will be a Safe place. *We* will be Safe.

Right?

As we move on to the next chapter, consider this: Safety is an *illusion*. Nothing more.

Does that feel uncomfortable? If you are a "normal" late twentieth-century North American, I expect it would feel uncomfortable. And that's OK, because Creativity is all about having Fun with the discomfort. And about . . . well, about just having Fun.

Chapter 3
"Having Fun with Fear!"

It's time to take another look at the *Cosmos/Chaos* chart.

Cosmos	Chaos
Order	Disorder
Structure	Random
Safe	Risk
Logical	Messy
Rules	Irrational
Expectations	Play
Game	Fun
Answers	Questions
Work	Letting Go
Control	Child
Adult	Creativity
Status Quo	New & Unknown

Notice that both Rules and Game are on the *Cosmos* side. So is Adult. Play, on the other hand, is on the *Chaos* side. Why?

Consider this: A toddler sits or stands in his or her crib or playpen. Along one of the top rails of the crib or playpen is a rod extending through several balls which can be slid back and forth on the rod. The toddler spends anywhere from minutes to hours moving the balls—sometimes in groups, sometimes individually—back and forth on the rod. Back and forth, back and forth, back and forth. (Does any of this sound familiar? Probably so.) All the while cooing, smiling, or squealing with glee.

Two questions: What are the Rules, and how does the toddler win? Obviously: 1) There aren't any, and 2) the toddler can't win. (Just as obviously, and perhaps more interestingly, neither can the toddler lose.)

The toddler is Playing. Games, on the other hand, are defined by (usually) very explicit and strict Rules. Why? So we can win. No Rules, no winning. It's that simple.

It is important that you understand I am less concerned about Games such as Monopoly®, horseshoes, and football. Of course, they certainly have a role in all this because we so often find ourselves counting on our football team (or horseshoe team) winning in order to validate us, to give us value. But I am more concerned with the interpersonal Games we play with (or against!) each other at home, at work, in relationships, or even with perfect strangers. (Dr. Eric Berne detailed many of these Games in his book, *Games People Play*.) In a quick and broad brush stroke, so many of these psychological Games come down to one-upmanship—I construct a Game with very intricate Rules, force you to take part in it (whether you know it or not), and do everything I can to make sure I win and you lose. Those are the really insidious Games, and we conduct them all the time.

Given all that, think about the concept of "Win/Lose" and on which side of the chart you think it belongs. I treat Win/Lose as one thing because I believe it is. It is a single concept, one aspect or side of which cannot exist without the other. They are cosmically and permanently fused into a single entity.

Because the Win/Lose concept is utterly dependent on Rules and Games and Order and Structure and such, I shamelessly and

ß

without hesitation put it on the *Cosmos* side of the chart. How about you?

So what is so darned important about the Win/Lose concept to spend a page or more on it? Again, that's simple. Winning makes us "Right"—proper, correct, appropriate, fitting, wholesome, righteous, etc., etc. . . . And there's hardly anything as important to us as being Right. Remember how important that was in school? During the last meeting at work? In your last conversation? Being Right validates us as valuable members of the society and the culture. Being Right makes us important and worthwhile.

Which leads to another concept-in-duality: the concept of "Right/Wrong." This is the same thing as Win/Lose. You can't have one without the other—they are a package. So where does this package, the concept of Right/Wrong, go on the chart? Consider that there is nothing disordered, Random, Messy, Irrational, Playful, or Childlike about it. No, it, unlike Play, is very Structured, Ordered, Rule-governed, and predictable.

If you think I'm hinting that Right/Wrong goes on the *Cosmos* side . . . I'm not hinting it, I'm saying it.

One way the Rules allow us to Win the Game and be Right is to quickly come up with the correct (or, at least, the most widely accepted) Answer. That's why we have learned to prefer Answers to Questions—Questions can't make us Right, but Answers can. An interesting dynamic is that of someone (everyone?) trying ever so hard to be invisible when Questions are being asked—whether in a classroom or a meeting or a casual conversation—except when one feels they have *THE Right Answer*. Then it's Nellie-bar-the-door, please, please, oh please call on (ask; recognize; listen to) me!

On the other hand, listen to a small Child some time (one able to talk, of course). They are *nothing but Questions*—why this, why that, how this, how that. Question after Question after Question. They aren't concerned with appearing stupid or Wrong (yet!). They just want to know, to learn. They're curious. Also, I'm not so sure they really care about the Answers all the time. Sometimes Questioning Adults until they (the Adults) go loopy can simply be Playing. Why? Because it's Fun.

55

It's time to take another look at the *Cosmos/Chaos* chart and see what we've added to it.

Cosmos	Chaos
Order	Disorder
Structure	Random
Safe	Risk
Logical	Messy
Rules	Irrational
Expectations	Play
Game	Fun
Answers	Questions
Work	Letting Go
Control	Child
Adult	Creativity
Status Quo	New & Unknown
Win/Lose	
Right/Wrong	

Visualize for a moment a horizontal scale on the chart above the words "Cosmos" and "Chaos". That scale indicates where a person—you, for instance—is on the chart. It describes your personality and explains many of the choices you find yourself making. Right now, you're probably somewhere—anywhere—left of center, biased toward the *Cosmos* side in your outlook toward and reactions to life. That's partly why you bought this book. At the same time, there are several things on the *Chaos* side you miss—Fun and Creativity large among them—and that you feel a true longing for. That's the other reason you bought this book.

I believe we all begin life deeply into *Chaos*, far to the right side of the chart. That's why I also believe we're all born Creative. But the teaching (and the learning; or, anyway, the accepting and believing) begins early: If we want to be a part of the world around us, no matter how grandly or intimately we wish to define that world, we must adopt the Rules of that world. And why do we want to belong? Because that is the ultimate Safety. Our greatest Fear is being alone in a cold and uncaring world. No, that's our second greatest Fear. Our greatest Fear is being actively banished, alone, to a cold and uncaring world. So what do we do? We start scooting to the *Cosmos* side. Sometimes we even up and run. We join in the Games with all their Rules. We become part of the system. We do our best to exert Control, work on Answers, do what's Expected, Win and have our Rightness validated, be an Adult . . . All so we will be Safe.

But in this quick-time scoot we leave a few things behind. Like Play and Fun and adventure. And Creativity.

Why? Fear. We're afraid.

What do we do to counteract this Fear? We seek to create Safety. How? By making every attempt and following every Rule to be Right, to Win.

At this point in the Workshop we do a little exercise to better understand what this means and where it gets us. I divide the workshop participants into pairs, and have each pair face one another standing up about a foot or so apart. They then raise their right arms and clasp hands as if they were about to arm wrestle, but with their elbows in midair. The instructions for the exercise are simple (as are all the instructions and exercises in the Workshop): Each person pushes the other person's arm over (just like arm wrestling) while verbally asserting, "I'm Right!" The other person then pushes the first's arm over and shouts, "No, *I'm* Right!" This continues, louder and louder, faster and faster, harder and harder. While they are all going at each other, I urge them on, reminding each of them how important it is for them to be Right, and how each of us devotes a lot of energy and time to doing exactly what they are doing right now— albeit usually not in so straightforward a way. And they Work at it, harder and faster and louder, until it really does become quite a contest.

That's when I tell them all to stop. As they stand there, some rubbing their arms and all looking a bit flushed, I suggest to them: "Kinda pointless, isn't it?" They usually agree. I also suggest: "And pretty much a waste of time?" Again they agree. "But," I point out, "this is what most of us do a lot of the time." We fight hard to be Right, to Win, so we can be Safe. And, yes, it is kinda pointless and a waste of time. As soon as you think you've made your point and assured your Rightness, another person takes it away from you as they assert their Rightness. As long as that is your focus, not only don't you truly *secure* your Rightness—and, therefore, Safety—but you also don't get anything else done.

The exercise is good at showing another problem on depending on Winning and being Right. Two interlinked problems, really. First, for you to be Right, you have to make someone else Wrong. Second, don't forget that while you're really focused on making someone else Wrong so you can be Right, someone else is out there really focused on making you—really *needing* to make you—Wrong, so *they* can be Right. That's a pretty dangerous battlefield, and certainly doesn't seem like the sort of place one would go to find Safety. Yet, that's what we do.

But Safety is an illusion: The Great Depression; Hurricane Andrew; drive-by shootings; "I shot an arrow into the air/It came to Earth I know not where;" fashion fads; another person's opinion and approval; the S&L debacle; DMSO; gold. As long as we seek Safety outside of ourselves—depend on external value systems and external situations—we are living an illusion. The Universe is a volatile place, and so are all its inhabitants. A good example is the "good luck piece" I was given by a friend years ago because I travelled so much. I still carry it around in my pocket today. It used to be a St. Christopher Medal, blessed by the Pope, no less. (Which Pope I don't remember.) Then one day I read in the newspaper that what I had was no longer a St. Christopher Medal, because St. Christopher was no longer a saint. Just Christopher (or Chris, whatever . . .). The Safety line that used to hold all my airplanes up was suddenly gone, and I didn't have a thing to say about it. I wasn't even asked.

By the way, I still carry the Christopher Medal around with me, because it was a gift from a friend and expressed that she really cared about me. I may not have believed in its "powers," but she did, and the fact that she wanted me to be Safe meant something to me. Still does. Oh, yeah: why do I carry it around in my pocket? The chain broke. See what I mean? Safety is an illusion.

So here we are, stuck on the horns of a temperamental dilemma: while feeling strongly that we should do everything we can to be Safe, we want to get back in touch with the Play and Fun that is our Creativity. Problem is, it's not Safe over there on that side of the chart where Creativity resides. In fact, that's where Risk is. Risk is the New & Unknown. Safety is the Status Quo. And, oh, how we seem to like the Status Quo. It may be a place full of devils, but

~~~~~

61

they are devils we know. We don't know what's in the New & Unknown. (That makes so much sense I won't even comment on it.) We may not like where we are, but we have spent time and energy building up a degree of what we like to think is Safety there. We are really uncomfortable with change. Mostly because we're afraid. So what do we do? We stay in the Status Quo and long for the New & Unknown.

I make workshop participants an offer. "How would you like a way," I ask them, "to be able to move to the New & Unknown without feeling that you must totally sever yourself from the Safety of the Structure you have in the Status Quo?" And they will all say, hesitating only a few seconds, "Sure." So I ask them to do this:

Get two large pieces of paper. Write in large letters on one piece: Status Quo. Write on the other piece in large letters: New & Unknown. When you're finished writing, place the two pieces of paper on the floor about 3 feet (or so) apart, and stand on the one that says, "Status Quo."

Simple enough, right? Why don't you do it, too. Get a couple of pieces of paper (8½ x 11, or so), a pencil, pen, crayon, magic marker, a lipstick, a piece of coal . . . Anyway, get something and write on one piece of paper "Status Quo" and on the other "New & Unknown." Write it large enough to be able to read it from a few feet away. When you're done, place the pieces of paper on the floor about 3 feet apart and stand on the one that says, "Status Quo."

I'll wait 'til you're ready.

We really do find ourselves too often caught between two strong motivators: we want to Play, but we're afraid to Risk. But just as Safety is illusory, I believe the condition of being "caught between" is illusory. When we were born, we were far to the right on the Cosmos/Chaos *chart. As we grew up and started believing certain external value systems and bought into their Structure, we moved to somewhere on the left side of the chart. The good news is that this illustrates* we can move back and forth, *left and right, on the scale. I further believe we can do it any time we want. But I get ahead of myself . . .*

OK, ready? I'll just tell you what I tell the Workshop participants. Imagine you're among twenty or more folks doing this. (As a matter of fact, it wouldn't hurt to ask a few people to join you in this exercise. They may not have the slightest idea of what you're doing or why you're asking them to do it too, but it might be Fun. Try it sometime.)

So here you are, smack-dab in the middle of your Status Quo, and wishing you had more Fun, more Play, more adventure in your life. You look around and see about 3 feet away something called New & Unknown. That's where you really want to go. But you are afraid. At least you know your way around your Status Quo. It's familiar there. To the extent you believe it possible to do so, you've made it Safe there. It's really hard to leave. It's not unlike a job or relationship or location or career that you've got a big stake in, but that you have lost interest in (to one degree or another). "Safe," predictable, reliable, Structured . . . boring. You really want the adventure, but, oh, are you afraid to leave. What if you don't like it in the New & Unknown? What if it doesn't work out? What if it isn't what you thought it would be, and it isn't what you want at all?

Well, you can "what if" it to death, but you'll never know until you go there. Soooo . . . when I say "Go," jump, hop, skip, step, slide, or otherwise get yourself over to the New & Unknown in two seconds or less. Ready? Go!

So here you are in the New & Unknown. And, oh my gosh, it isn't anything like what you expected or, worse, wanted. It's scary, it's frightening, it's threatening, it's lonely, and it's just so generally higgledy-piggledy that part of you really regrets taking the leap. What's a person to do?

Take a look around the floor near you. Do you see close by a piece of paper that was your Status Quo? Still there, isn't it? Well, here comes the really simple part. When I say "Go," jump, hop, skip, step, slide, or otherwise get yourself back to your Status Quo. Ready? Go!

Whew! Got out of that buckaroo bonzo New & Unknown just in time. And it's just that simple. How simple? Do it again: Over to New & Unknown. Now back to Status Quo. And again. And again. See? Simple. So simple, in fact, that moving over to the New & Unknown isn't so scary any more, is it?

"But, whoa!" you say. "I don't like my job at Western Widgets waxing wedges. Are you trying to tell me if I leave that job and head off on a Big Adventure into the New & Unknown at another job or line of work, then find I don't like it, that the folks back at

W.W. are ready to welcome me back to my old job, my old Status Quo? Wait just a darn minute!"

No, I don't really believe you could waltz right back into Western Widgets. But ask yourself: Is it Western Widgets you really wanted to leave, or was it a situation in where you felt unfulfilled, unappreciated (especially by yourself), unexcited, stifled, bored, or otherwise simply unhappy? If you didn't feel that way, you probably wouldn't have gone off looking in the first place. And if that *really* is what you left—and not Western Widgets per se—well, I believe you can find any number of situations where you will feel unfulfilled, unappreciated (especially by yourself), unexcited, stifled, bored, or otherwise simply unhappy. So, yes, you can return to your old Status Quo. You can go back to feeling miserable anytime you want. Simple.

"Simple" brings up another point. Thinking back to the *Cosmos/Chaos* chart, where would you put "Simple" and "Complex"? And while you're at it, where would you put "Fear" and "Adventure"?

Here's where I think they go:

Cosmos	Chaos
Order	Disorder
Structure	Random
Safe	Risk
Logical	Messy
Rules	Irrational
Expectations	Play
Game	Fun
Answers	Questions
Work	Letting go
Controlling	Child
Adult	Creativity
Status Quo	New & Unknown
Win/Lose	**Simple**
Right/Wrong	**Fear**
Complex	**Adventure**

Why? (Good Question—Childlike, curious.) Because there is nothing Complex about Chaos. It simply is. Cosmos, on the other hand, is defined and Controlled by more and more Complex layers of Rules and Structure. Ever read *all* the Rules printed on the inside of the box lid of a Monopoly® game? Whew! But where is the Complexity in the situation with the toddler and the balls on his or her crib rail? Only in our Adult minds as we try to make sense and Order out of what the toddler is doing. In fact, some Adult minds—such as those of the parents of the toddler—might go to some lengths to construct a Complex reason why what the toddler (*their* toddler, the result of *their* gene commingling) is doing proves how bright, smart, advanced, gifted, etc., the toddler is. They are attempting to overlay a Complex scenario to create Right and Win—*for themselves*, not the kid. The kid knows better: it's Play and it's Fun. Thank heavens that kid doesn't know he or she has already been entered in the Game, and that to survive (emotionally, at least) he or she must be Right and Win. He or she may just decide right then and there to never grow up and have no truck at all with such folly, thank you very much.

If you get the feeling that Playing is a key to getting in touch with your innate Creative power, you are right on track. If you also sense that dealing with the Risk and Fear that go along with Play and Creativity is key, you're further down the right track.

Speaking of Playing and Risking and Fun and track, do you suppose many people would pay good money (as opposed to bad money?) and stand in line to ride a *flat* roller coaster? Nope, didn't think you would. Neither do I. It's interesting that we would accept that element of Risk, and face that level of Fear to have Fun on a roller coaster, but shy away from it when Playing becomes really important. And, believe me, it becomes really important when we want to be as Creative as we have the potential to be.

The roller coaster is an interesting example because of something most folks do on a roller coaster to *enhance* the thrill and, therefore, the Fun: They Let Go. Just as the roller coaster goes into free fall—the point at which any sense of Safety would dictate that a rider hold on even harder—they Let Go.

And Letting Go—which you will please notice is on the *Chaos* side of the chart—is the key that fits the lock to the door that opens up the Playroom. The difference between Game and Play is surrender

—surrendering the need for the Rules and Structure that create Win/Lose and Right/Wrong.

Letting Go doesn't mean that the Fear goes away and that the Risk isn't there anymore. If it did, then Letting Go of the bar in the roller coaster would flatten out the track. No, Letting Go means: I know there's a Risk, and *it's alright that there is Fear*. Letting Go means you don't have to be Right, you don't have to Win. Letting Go means you'd rather Play. Letting Go means you opt for a helter-skelter luge ride through the Alps of your mind and your world and you don't know for sure where the brake is. What you *are* sure of is that you're going to end up somewhere else, somewhere you may never have been, and you're in for an Adventure, gathering new data points and reconnecting them at a speed that makes a particle accelerator look like a lazy Sunday carousel. Letting Go means *working within your Fear*, not letting your Fear Control where, when, and how you go and don't go.

And, what the heck, if you don't like where you've been on that luge ride and where you end up, you can always lug it back up the mountain whence you came and use it as a bench upon which to sit as you gaze out toward where you'd like to go and curse where you are. You can always go back to being miserable again.

A quick aside, if you will allow me. Well, heck, I'm writing this, so even if you don't allow me. During some TV coverage of one Winter Olympics or another I heard the following as a commentator was filling time during the luge competition: "The luge is an excellent example of man's [Adult man's, I presume; PJ] ability to Complicate even the Simplest things." Speaks volume's, doesn't it? Then there was the news report on a show of inventions by children. Concerning one of them, a rather clever one, the reporter said it was "so Simple, only a Child would have thought of it." Hmmm . . . But more on that in a moment.

How do you improve your ability to work within your Fear? Here are a couple of Workshop exercises designed for that.

The first is really Simple. Well, they both are, come to think of it. And they both are exercises best done with other people. So invite some friends over, ditch the charades, and try these.

〰

刀

First: Word Association. You remember that one. If you haven't done it before, you've seen it used in almost every B-grade 1950-60's psychology/psychiatry film every made. In the Workshop I get everyone sitting on the floor in a circle, with me standing in the middle. I tell the group how the exercise works, who will start, and in what direction it will go. Here's how it works: I choose one person —Sally, for instance—and tell her I will say a word to her and tell her it will go to her left (for instance). What she must do as quickly as possible is turn to the person on her left—Tom, for instance—and say to Tom the very first thing that came to her mind when I said my word to her. Tom then turns to his left—to, uh, Bridget?—and says to her the very first thing that came to his mind when Sally said her word to him. Simple, huh?

Well, it doesn't start out that way. Here are some of the things that happen: Sally takes forever to "think" of a word in response to my word. She then says that word to the carpet in the middle of the circle. Tom reacts to Sally's word by looking up at me and saying his word with a question mark after it. Bridget hears Tom's word and I can see her immediately reject—for whatever reason—the first thing that comes to her mind and think up something else which she then passes on to Bert. Bert then looks me squarely in the eye and says a word in reaction to either the word I gave Sally or the one she said to the floor. Etc., etc., etc. . . .

So what's going on here? Several things. First off, few folks begin this exercise by Playing. They think its a Game to be Won or Lost, and they all want to be Right. Sally probably considered the first thing that came to her mind, mulled it over, but wasn't really able to determine, given the vague "Rules of Engagement," whether it was or wasn't Right, figured she was going to Lose, and just let her word fall as inconspicuously as possible to the floor instead of saying it directly to Tom. Tom wasn't sure if he was Right either, so he "asked" his word to me, as if to say, "Is that Right?" How should I know—I wasn't in his head when he heard Sally's word. Bridget edited. She was certain the first thing she thought of was Wrong or stupid or silly, and she didn't want others to think of her that way. So, she came up with another much more reasonable, sensible, correct, Adult (she thought) response. And Bert? Of course, he, along with everyone else, heard the word I gave Sally to start things off. And as soon as he did, he had what he thought was a terrific response word. So he waited, ears and mind closed, until it was his

~~~~~

73

turn. Then he responded to *me* and *my* word, not to Bridget's or Tom's or even Sally's. He was much like the kid we all had in one class or another in school who just *knew* they had the Right Answer and begged to be called upon so he could deliver that Right Answer in front of everyone and Win the Game.

In other words, few—if any—follow instructions and do the exercise the first time or two. They edit, they try to Win by being Right, they figure they're going to Lose so they give up. Nobody Plays. Well, practically nobody. They don't Let Go.

I tell them what they're doing. Then I change the focus a bit. I challenge them to get completely around the circle in 20 seconds or less. I stand in a far corner of the room and tell them that I must be able to hear each of them. These two factors are important. The point is to put their physical energy into the Simple act, and not in the Complex intellectualizing.

I tell them to listen only to the person giving them a word, and to speak directly to the person to whom they are giving a word. And I remind them that this is Play, not a game. Quit trying to do it Right, and just *do it*!

What happens? It gets better, faster, sillier, and becomes Fun. They begin to Let Go, Risk saying something stupid or embarrassing, stop keeping score, and start to Play. They also begin to realize that the Simpler they keep it, the better it works.

We need to be reminded of that, because as Adults we love to Complicate things. I believe making things more Complex than they really need to be is something we do to validate the importance of our Adulthood, our "Adultness." We worked hard to get our Adulthood membership card. We paid heavy dues. It's really scary to think that it may be worth less than we paid. So we protect our Adulthood by making it Complex. If everything were really Simple, why did we pay so much—why did we leave so much Fun and Simplicity and Play behind—to be recognized as an Adult? Am I really that stupid? If I am, I don't want anyone to know it, because then I Lose. So I'll make it Complex, so Complex only I understand it. Then I'm important and valuable, not stupid and worthless. Boy, this being an Adult is a tough job, and certainly not Simple. Right?

The second of these exercises is a lot of Fun—that is, when those taking the Workshop decide to let it be Fun. I call it Motor-Mouth. Here's how it works:

Another circle, but this time with everyone standing. I choose an "official timer" and an "official score keeper." The timer is armed with a stopwatch I make sure to have on hand. The score keeper is armed with a piece of chalk. I give the group the instructions: Everyone will have a turn, even the timer and the score keeper. When it is your turn, I will give you a subject and then say "Go!" The timer starts the stop watch and you must talk continuously for 30 seconds without saying "uh," "um," or "you know," or pausing for more than two seconds. Everyone whose turn it *isn't* (including me) is charged with listening for an "uh," "um," "you know," or a pause of more than two seconds. If any of those is heard, those who hear it are to yell or scream or make some sort of obnoxious noise not unlike the buzzer on a game show, and the timer stops the stopwatch and tells the score keeper how long the person went—five seconds, or 20 seconds, or whatever. If you make it to 30 seconds, the timer yells out, "Thirty!" The score keeper writes the time on the board next to the person's name. Before the end of the exercise the timer and the score keeper take their turns, being replaced in their official duties by two others who have already had a turn.

Got all that? It's simple, really. And it tends to scare the cheese right out of everyone. Of course, I ask for volunteers, and, of course, I then have to select who will start (and usually most of those who follow). I choose subjects ranging from the negative social effects of railroad hotboxes, to why some podiatrists actually *prefer* that women wear high heel shoes, to the strategic importance of submarine screw cavitation signatures, to the more obvious drawbacks unique to digital sound reproduction. One thing I do in choosing subjects is sometimes to match up a subject with a person who probably knows something about it, and sometimes to match up a subject with a person who I am fairly certain will know nothing about it.

I think the best single word to describe the exercise—from the participants' points of view—is dread. At that particular moment all of them would much rather be anywhere else on the planet— including the gallery of the United States Senate—than in the Workshop. Why? Fear, pure and simple. There's no getting out of it this time. Each of them is dead certain he or she is about to make

〰〰

a big spotted and speckled, A-1, ta-rah-rah-boom-dee-ay FOOL out of himself or herself. And in front of everyone else. Good Lord and Kleenex®, there's no way out!

Workshop participants usually approach the exercise with one of three points of view: 1) If I'm lucky, I'll get a subject I know about and I'll Win (I usually give them a subject I think they know something about); 2) I'm not going to make it, I'm gonna die, I hate my parents, let's get it over with (I usually give them a subject I think they know little or nothing about); and 3) Ah, what the heck, let's Play (the subject doesn't matter).

So how does it work out? The 1)'s usually don't make it past ten seconds. The 2)'s sometimes crash after two seconds, and sometimes make it all the way to 30 seconds. The 3)'s almost always make it to 30 seconds (and beyond, if I don't stop them). Why? Because this exercise has nothing to do with being Right. In fact, just like "Connect the Dots" (remember: all I say is "connect the dots."), I never tell anyone they have to speak on the subject I give them. I just tell them I'm going to give them a subject. Those who think they *must* speak on their given subject are following their own *implied rules*. They still think the point is to be smart and Right and to Win. The 3)'s, on the other hand, are willing to Let Go, take on the Risk of seeming to be foolish, work within their Fear, and *Play*. They focus on the very simple task at hand: don't say "uh," "um," "you know," or pause for more than two seconds. And, hold me Hannah, they somehow are able to go from the applications of algorithms to the Gettysburg Address complete with Zipcode to the tendency of a donkey to have unequal ear lengths. One even went so far as to just recite their address over and over and over until the 30 seconds were up.

So what's the point? Practice working within your Fear. Practice Letting Go. Remember how much Fun it is to Play. It's all very Simple—and even easy—if you are willing to see Safety as an illusion, and if you're willing to set aside your need to Win and be Right. The only way out of Fear is through it. You can only go through it if you are willing to Let Go. Letting your Fear keep you from moving is endless terror. Letting Go of the Safety rail and screaming like a banshee in a bad horror film as the roller coaster goes over and down the big one is FUN!

Chapter 4

"Look at it this way . . . And this way . . ."

Take another look at the *Cosmos/Chaos* chart and see if something doesn't just sort of jump out at you.

Cosmos	Chaos
Order	Disorder
Structure	Random
Safe	Risk
Logical	Messy
Rules	Irrational
Expectations	Play
Game	Fun
Answers	*Questions*
Work	Letting Go
Controlling	Child
Adult	Creativity
Status Quo	New & Unknown
Win/Lose	Simple
Right/Wrong	Fear
Complex	Adventure

Isn't it amazing, the way that happens! Anyway, yes, the point is where you find Questions and where you find Answers. What you've learned over the years is that there is One Right Answer, and if you want to Win you must get to that One Right Answer as quickly as possible. Problem is, Answer is not where Creativity is. That's because Creativity is curious. In fact, *insatiably* curious. Curiosity fuels Creativity by constantly finding new data points, and new ways to connect them.

And *any* Question can have more than one Right Answer. It all depends on how you ask the Question. The person who is really using their Creative power finds all sorts of ways to ask any given Question, all sorts of different ways to look at it and interpret it. Here's an example: how many different ways can you find to "ask" the following Question to produce different Answers? How many different ways can you look at this Question:

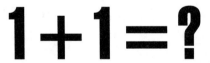

Think about it for a moment. Write down all the different perfectly good Answers you can come up with for this Question. I'll wait.

This is a process I call "Hanging Out In The Question." If you Let Go of the need to be Right so you can Win, you can stay and frolic with any Question for as long as you want. And the more you Hang Out In The Question, the more Answers you find. And isn't that more Fun, really, having more than One Right Answer to choose from? Imagine your disappointment if you walked into a restaurant, opened the menu, and saw only one thing—like . . . I don't know . . . tomato aspic—listed. Certainly, if the thing you wanted most from a restaurant at that moment was tomato aspic, you're in luck. But, come on, what are the odds? Even if you liked *tomato aspic, you'd be disappointed that* you didn't have a choice.

Hanging Out In The Question—looking at it from many different ways and asking it in many different ways—allows you to create a pretty fair menu of Answers. Now you've got a choice of several perfectly good Answers. And it's Fun.

So what did you come up with? How many perfectly good Answers did you find for the Question "1+1=?" How about: 1+1=2. Why not? It's a perfectly good Answer. The obvious is just as valid as the hidden (or: Yet to be discovered). The key is not to stop there. How about: 1+1=11. Whoa! How? (Sounds like an old cowboy movie.) Simple—when you put a 1 with another 1 you have an 11. How about: 1+1=3. Who said this was math? I just said the statement was a Question. So maybe the Question is asking what happens when two beings ("1" and "1") procreate? Being good begetters, they beget an offspring. " . . . and baby makes three," as the old song goes. And so on.

How many more did you come up with? How many more do you think you could come up with now? All you need to do is Hang Out In The Question a little longer.

One of the best ways I know of to Hang Out In The Question is to look at the Question in a different way. To change perspective. Literally. As human beings we tend to look at the world and most everything in it from one physical point of view: eye level. If you have a small Child, or a dog, or a cat, imagine how your house or apartment (or whatever) looks to them. When is the last time you went around your home looking at it the way your cat sees it? If you did, what would it look like? How might it change your impressions of things like your TV and your sofa?

When is the last time you looked at the underside of whatever passes as your dining room table? Have you ever looked straight down at the top of your house and yard (or whatever)? What does a car look like to a street? What does a tree look like to a bird?

How can it be that from your car you see a freeway that's real wide, but that same freeway seen from an airliner at cruising altitude is a long, skinny line? Your perspective has changed, of course. You can create an ever-growing menu of Answers by doing the same thing with Questions—look at them from a different point of view, from several, in fact. The more different views, the more Answers (just like dot-connection patterns) you see. As soon as you feel you've exhausted one point of view, don't immediately settle for one of those Answers. Change your point of view. STAY IN THE QUESTION! Be willing to take the Risk of not having the One Right Answer before everyone else. You'll be surprised by how many more—and usually *better*—Answers you can come up with in a very short time. But only if you keep asking the Question by looking at it from lots of different angles, and not jumping right to an Answer.

The more you practice changing points of view, you *automatically* become more curious—about everything. In fact, you're on the way to being insatiably curious. One way to practice changing your point of view, switching your perspective, is this simple little quiz:

Take a piece of paper and a pen or pencil and in three minutes write down everything you can think that thing up there is. Go ahead . . . I'll wait.

I've used this well-known little quiz on both Children and Adults in the Workshop. It has been used by educators, psychologists, creativity gurus, and many others lots of times. And it's always Fun to see what happens.

How did you do? Was it easy? Did you edit? Did you find yourself writing down a list of similar things, or was your list all over the map? Well, here's what happens in the Workshop:

Some people are hard put to see it as even ten different things. That's usually because they keep looking at it in the same way. They haven't quite Let Go. They still believe in a Right Answer instead of just Answers, each as Right as the others. Some people fill up the page with possibilities. They're lookin' and cookin', turning the page either in their hands or their minds, squinting with one eye, then the other—they're *exploring* lots of possibilities. Most folks are somewhere in between, and while they do entertain different possibilities, they spend most of their time at "eye level."

What I have found is this: The single most popular Answer among Adults is "dot." Next is "spot," and next is "period." Children's papers are also peppered with dots, spots, and periods, but that just seems to be a starting place. They then go on to write things like "the top of a flag pole." Wow, what a change in perspective! And then there was: "A black sun in a white universe." Whew! Another one of my favorites, from an eleven-year-old: "This is a drop of ink that fell from the quill pen Thomas Jefferson was using when he signed the Declaration of Independence." What unbridled Fun! And, of course, this from a teenager: "A zit." It figures.

The more different ways you look at any one thing, the more things it can be. The more different ways you ask the Question, the larger your menu of Answers to choose from. Don't be so eager to leave the Question. Staying there not only gives you more Answers, but it can be a lot of Fun, too. Because it's Play. And it's Creative.

Now that you've got a better sense of looking at things from new and different angles and not taking them at face value, how about another pop quiz? What follows, word for word, is one I use in the Workshop.

> The following numbers have been arranged systematically:
>
> **8,5,4,9,1,7,6,3,2,0**
>
> What is the system?

Take two minutes—as if you really needed all that time—and figure it out. Let me know when you've got it.

While you're figuring, a few Questions. Are you still looking at the page straight on? Have you flipped it over, or on edge? Have you looked at it from far away, or from up close? Remember, this is all about looking at things—Questions—from different perspectives.

Dum-dee-dum-dum-dum . . . All done? Got it figured out? No? OK, be honest—was subtracting 5 from 8 the first thing you did, which gave you 3? And then 4 from 5, giving you 1? And then 9 from 4, giving you –5? And you couldn't see a pattern, a system, so you figured that wasn't the system? Is that the first thing you did? If so, you're right in there with over 90% of the Workshop participants. But, nope, that's not the system.

How about: ten numbers separated from one another by commas? Wellll . . . That's *a* system, but it's not *THE* system.

Simple random sequence? Nope.

Look again, and remember that this is all about *changing your perspective*. Anything? Hmmm . . . OK, I'll give you a big hint:

Read the numbers out loud. Go ahead. Read them out loud. Yep, that's the hint.

Dum-dee-dum-dum-dum . . . Got it yet?

Are you ready to groan and have your head fall into your hands? OK, here goes:

The numbers are in alphabetical order. (Groan!!!)

Change your perspective. Why must a system for arranging numbers be numerical? Yes, it is Expected that it be numerical. Assuming it is so is the Logical, Ordered, *Safe* thing to do. Goodness knows we don't want to be caught looking for a numbering system that isn't numerical—people would think we were pretty darn silly.

But if the point is to explore different perspectives, doesn't it make perfect sense, after the "numerical" possibilities have been exhausted, to look at some system that hasn't a thing to do with numbers? Of course it does. And why stop at alphabetical? When you've got some time on your hands and it's a bad TV night, see if you can't find still another system. Look at it from another direction, another perspective.

A terrific example of a collision of different perspectives—and of the fact that two *very* different perspectives can exist relative to the same subject at the same time—is the true story of a friend of mine back in the mid-70's. He was the father of a twosomething boy, and a subscriber to *Playboy* magazine. One weekend afternoon he walked out of his kitchen to find his son standing next to the coffee table where he had left the latest *Playboy* edition. Naturally, the young lad had opened the magazine to the centerfold, and had even opened up the centerfold to full length. In an instant, the father panicked, thinking: "Heavens, it's way too early to start explaining these sorts of things to my son. Why, oh, why did I leave that magazine there? Well, maybe it won't make much sense to him, and when I walk into the room it will distract him and I can wait another decade or so before we have a little chat. Yeah, that's the ticket," he reasoned, full of both hope and despair. But, as he entered the living room, his heart sank to the basement next to the water heater, all because his son looked up at his approaching father, pointed at the varnished vixen on the page and opened his mouth to speak. The father froze. His heart hid behind the hot water heater. And the son said, "Look, Daddy! She isn't wearing any shoes!"

It isn't too tough to imagine that the father and the son had different perspectives when it came to looking at women, clothed or otherwise. A twosomething's eye level is just about at Adults' knees. So they concentrate on, and take very seriously, things like feet. The father's eye level was a bit higher.

Different perspectives of the same thing allow you to see many different things, even though what you're looking at doesn't change. Hang Out In The Question longer, and you'll soon be developing huge menus of perfectly good Answers.

Developing those menus, and asking the Question in many different ways, and even challenging whether the Question put forth is really the Question that needs an Answer, are, as I see it, all part of what author/lecturer/teacher/consultant Edward De Bono calls "Lateral Thinking." (Also known by some as "Horizontal Thinking" and "Zigzag Thinking.") It works something like this:

Most vertical, or straight line, thinkers, when faced with a Question, insist on an Answer ASAP, and they insist on *that* Question yielding the Answer, the One Right Answer. So, as if they were all medieval battering rams, they bang their heads against the door of the Question until the door opens or their heads crack and their brains fall out. The horizontal, or zigzag, thinker, on the other hand, can take a hint a lot faster and has more respect for his or her brains. So he (or she) asks: "What other ways are there to do this? To do what? Do I want to open the door, or to get inside? How many different ways are there to do either, or both?" He (or she) may appear in a muddle, but is actually much more likely to reach his (or her . . . whatever) goal than the head-crackers. And, in the process, he (whatever . . .) is much more apt to fully understand what his (. . .) goal really is. (What a bonus!)

Here's an example of how it works:

A high-rise office building is built, and the tenant businesses move in. Right away employees from all the businesses start complaining about how slow the elevators are. They feel they are spending inordinate amounts of time waiting on the ground floor to go up to their offices, and in the many floor lobbies to go back down. The complaints become serious, affecting morale.

So the managers of the businesses go to the building management and demand a solution—a real, lasting solution. Now, this poses a difficult problem. Replacing the elevators with faster models would be prohibitively expensive. So would installing additional elevators, not to mention the fact that the building was not designed to contain them. Nor could they put additional elevators on the outside of the building without spending a bunch of bucks and ruining the building's esthetics. What to do, what to do . . .

But they were good horizontal thinkers, so they spent some time with the Question. Among other things they did as they explored different perspectives, different points of view, was to investigate the Question: Was the problem the elevators, or the people? It could be expressed either way, of course. But having exhausted elevator solutions, they went on to consider the people ones. As a result of Hanging Out In The Question, looking at it from many different perspectives, they built up an impressive menu of Answers. And from that menu, they chose the elegantly Simple one:

They lined the elevator lobbies on every floor with mirrors. (Egad, I love it!)

You can probably guess what happened. The employees were now so distracted by looking at themselves and each other in the mirrors, they lost track of how long their wait was. They thought the elevators had been speeded up!

Why does Horizontal Thinking work so well? That's simple. It's because Horizontal Thinking is:

- Risking being Wrong.

- Hanging Out In The Question.

- Playing, considering more than One Right Answer.

- Connecting the dots over and over again and *not* stopping at the first possible solution.

- Giving yourself permission to use the Creative power you already have, believing in it, trusting it (now *that's* Risky).

So what is the point? There are always many points of view when dealing with any Question. And each different point of view, each different perspective, is another Question. And each of the Questions has any number of perfectly good Answers. The point is to use whatever works for you, whatever allows you to Hang Out In

The Question for as long as possible, so you can fill out a massive menu of Answers to choose from instead of rushing headlong and straight arrow, blinders on, toward the first, the only, the One Right Answer. It's Risky, because others might come up with *an* Answer before you and claim they have Won. But don't worry—in the end, you'll come up with *better* Answers, and have a lot of Fun along the way.

Chapter pop quiz #1:

So, what's *your* point of view?

Chapter pop quiz (exercise, really) #2:

Sometimes the best way to practice Hanging Out In The Question is to ask a Question for which there is no ready Answer. It's also a good way to exercise Risking not having an Answer. It's also a good way to develop *insatiable* curiosity. And it's also Fun. Try these, then add some more of your own:

- Why are "stop" and "high" the same word ("alto") in Spanish?

- Why is baseball the only sport that penalizes the offense if they touch the ball?

- What would the world be like if people were two feet tall and six feet wide?

- Why do we drive on a parkway, and park on a driveway?

- Why is "abbreviated" such a long word?

- When they ship styrofoam, what do they pack it in?

- Since bread always lands buttered side down, and a cat always lands on its feet, what happens when you butter some bread, strap it on the back of a cat, and throw the cat up in the air?

- Why are there no International House of Pancakes® *outside* the United States?

Chapter 5

"Creating the perfect balance."

— or —

"Creating: The perfect balance."

W hat is the difference between "Gaming" and "Playing"? What is the difference between "Questions" and "Answers"? What is the difference between "Safety" and "Risk"? What is the difference between all the stuff on the *Cosmos* side of the chart, and all the stuff on the *Chaos* side?

Take another look at the chart and think about it for a moment.

Cosmos	Chaos
Order	Disorder
Structure	Random
Safe	Risk
Logical	Messy
Rules	Irrational
Expectations	Play
Game	Fun
Answers	Questions
Work	Letting Go
Controlling	Child
Status Quo	New & Unknown
Adult	Creativity
Win/Lose	Simple
Right/Wrong	Fear
Complex	Adventure

That's right: most everything on the *Cosmos* side is an END (or: an end result), while The *Chaos* stuff is PROCESS (or: ongoing, unfinished). Which means that Creativity is a Process. It never Ends. There is always another way to ask the Question. But where we find ourselves most often is at the End, or at least focusing on it.

Decades ago, my father taught me something important about the difference between the End and the Process, and, whether he knew it or not, sensitized me to how End-focused most of us are. He had taken me as a ten-year-old to my first baseball game—Yankee Stadium, New York City. 'Long about the sixth or seventh inning, when my fascination with hot dogs, cotton candy, and the way my father ate the peanuts with the shells still on them had worn off, I decided to ask what was up on the field (I hadn't a clue). So I turned to my still-shelled-peanut-eating father and asked: "Who's winning?" "No one," he said, popping another packaged pair of peanuts in his mouth. "The game isn't over yet. But the Yankees are *leading*." The game was IN PROCESS. It had not yet come to an END. Sorta like Creativity. Sorta like life. A lot like life, in fact.

(I don't know if he intended to teach me something as profound as this, but I like to think he did. Thanks, Dad.)

The good news from this is that yes, indeed, life itself is Process, and is not an End. No matter how far to the *Cosmos* side of the chart you may have gone, it doesn't have to End there. Whenever you choose to take on the Risks and uncertainties of the *Chaos* side, and Let Go of the (illusion of) Safety you've gone to such trouble to construct by following the Rules of the Game in order to Win and be Right, you can scoot right back to the *Chaos* side. You can unlock your Creative power anytime you want. All you have to do is get back in touch with somcone—someone you know, and who has waited patiently for you all this time. That someone is there on the chart. Do you see who it is?

Your Child.

It is that part of you that was born Creative, but was pushed back and pushed back by a learned belief in Safety until it seemed to be there no more. But that part of you that is the Child you were and are *is still there*, fully functional and ready to Play, ready to Create. There is nothing Creative about your Adult—that part of you that has taken on all the trappings of the Adult world around you. Useful, sure: your Adult is as practical as pliers, and often as necessary. But it is not Creative. Your Child is the Creative part of you. The power of your Creativity is limited only by your willingness to join your Child in Play.

But before you tear up your credit cards and start rummaging through the pantry for some Ovaltine®, hold up there. The point of this book or of the Workshop is not to get you to body slam yourself against the far right side of the chart. The point is much the same as Hanging Out In The Question: creating the largest possible menu of possibilities. If that is the case (and, indeed, it is), where on the chart do you think it's best to be?

Take a look.

Cosmos	**Chaos**
Order	Disorder
Structure	Random
Safe	Risky
Logical	Messy
Rules	Irrational
Expectations	Play
Game	Fun
Answers	Questions
Work	Letting Go
Controlling	Child
Adult	Creativity
Win/Lose	Simple
Right/Wrong	Fear
Complex	Adventure

That's right: smack-dab in the center. Why? That's Simple. It's the easiest place from which to be able to access *all* the stuff on the whole chart. Why limit yourself? It's not about regressing, abandoning your Adult and totally becoming your Child again. It's about embracing your Child shamelessly, guiltlessly, happily, so you, as both Adult *and* Child, can look at the world and all the Questions in it *from both points of view*.

Considering that Right/Wrong and, therefore, Good/Bad are over on the *Cosmos* side and Creativity (and Child and Play and Risk, etc.) are on the *Chaos* side, how do you judge if you are really Letting Go—I mean *really* Letting Go—and Playing with your Child and, as a result, fully tapping your Creative power? What measure do you use? How do you judge?

There are two ways, and the first involves another little story.

Once upon a time . . . Oops. Wrong story.

A guest lecturer—a business entrepreneur well known for his successes—addressed a large group of MBA candidates at the University of Utah. After his talk, all the students left the lecture hall save three. Those three hung back to get a moment alone with the guest lecturer. They complimented him on his address, and then asked if he could boil it all down to its essence and tell them one thing: What is the secret to success?

"Simple," he said (sound familiar?). He picked up a piece of chalk, turned, and wrote on the board behind him. He pointed to the board and said to the three: "*That* is the secret to success." He had written one word on the board, in very large letters. The word was this: PASSION.

Since Creativity—and, yes, life itself—is a Process and not an End, do not measure it by the result, which is an End. Measure it—judge it, if you will—by the passion of your Process. Just how passionately do you accept all the Risks? How passionately do you embrace your Child? A person who is passionate about what they want to do Simply does it. One who is not passionate about it traps himself or herself in *trying* to do it. In fact, their passion is spent in/on the trying, not the doing.

And here is the other way to measure, to judge your Process: Honesty. Passion and Creativity are not Good or Bad, Right or Wrong. They are Simply honest or dishonest. Either you are passionate, or you aren't. Either you use your Creative power, or you don't. Either you are willing to Let Go, Risk, Play, and forget Win/Lose, or you're not. Being honest is really very Simple. Being Dishonest is usually quite Complex. "Oh, what a tangled web we weave/When first we practice to deceive."—remember?

In this very Adult (*Cosmos*) world of ours, honesty is something else: Very precious, because it is so rare. I would like to suggest, though, that you are worth it. Your Child is worth it. Honesty is something you deserve. Thankfully, it is something you can give yourself whenever you decide to. And without it, how will you ever know just how Creatively powerful you really are?

Besides giving you a very handy way to stay in touch with your *Chaos* side, honesty does something else for you: It lets you know what you *Want*. To consciously and honestly *know* what you Want is a very important and, regrettably, an often difficult thing to do. Why? Because you have been taught for so long and by so many that Wanting is selfish, and selfish is Wrong. So as long as you are into Right/Wrong, Win/Lose, you will avoid like the plague *appearing* to be selfish. The result? You set your sights on what you *Should* Want instead of what you *do* Want. Which means that if you are successful, you end up with what other people have determined you Want, not what you Want. You repress Want and put in its place Should. Because those are the Rules. That's the way the Game is played. That's how you Win.

Which means now the chart looks like that over there:

Cosmos	Chaos
Order	Disorder
Structure	Random
Safe	Risk
Logical	Messy
Rules	Irrational
Expectations	Play
Game	Fun
Answers	Questions
Work	Letting Go
Control	Child
Status Quo	New & Unknown
Adult	Creativity
Win/Lose	Simple
Right/Wrong	Fear
Complex	Adventure
End	**Process**
Should	**Want**

Should is an Adult word, one that imposes limits and lines you must color within. Want is a Child word, one that is passionate and honest. To unlock your Creative power, you need to be able to tell the difference between these two. And, yes, there will be many times when you will follow the Shoulds in the world, mostly because there is an Adult part of you existing in an Adult world. The point is not to abandon either Should or Want. The point is to be honest with yourself and *always know the difference between the two.*

Passion and Want interact rather interestingly. Once you've identified what you Want, you know where to direct your passion. Conversely, if you find it truly difficult to be passionate about something, then it probably isn't what you really Want and is more likely something you believe you *Should* Want. It's a nice barometer.

It has been my experience that what makes honestly answering the Question "What do I Want?" so often difficult is not that you don't know deep in your soul what it is. It's that you don't really think you're worthy of having it. That, of course, is the result of a lot of stuff you've been "told" and you believed since you were very young. It can be a very tough subject, and one which deserves a book of its own—as if it didn't have oodles of them already. Just thought I'd bring it up. Another Question just left hanging there . . .

A very convenient thing about reaching a balance in the middle of the chart, as I have already said, is that it makes reaching down into one side just as easy as reaching down into the other. This is of crucial importance if your Adult and Child are going to have equal importance in your life and how you live it. It's also darn handy when you have to get past Fear and Risk to get to Creativity. Why? Because there is something Safe to hold on to.

Just as your Status Quo didn't disappear when you stepped to the New & Unknown (it just became, ultimately, less and less attractive and had less and less of a "hold" on you), you can, if you need to, put a little piece of Safety in your pocket as you face Risk and Fear. How? Glad you asked.

Have you ever experienced one of those terrible situations when you (especially your ego) was at such risk that you stopped and looked heavenward, saying "Lord, if you're going to take me, take me *now*, because I'm never going to make it through this?" Of course, it doesn't have to be literally that. I just like to express those moments—however long or short—in that way. What it really means is this: Your ego is faced with something so frightening and so threatening to your ego and its survival that you truly believe you can't make it through intact (emotionally). You would much rather shrink to the size of an atom and fall through a crack somewhere. You want to just disappear instead of having to continue to face whoever is present, even if it is only you. You have just proven to them—and to the world—that you are a dolt, an imbecile, an idiot. Or you have just realized—through thought or action or reaction—that *they were Right all along: you're not worthy!* All you want to do is die. Poof! Right then and there. Whatever your Fears of dying, they are *nothing* compared to yours Fears of continuing on in this particular situation.

It can be as (relatively) harmless as this one incident related in a Workshop. A young woman was telling of the time when she was the master of ceremonies at a large dinner. For the occasion, she was wearing a fairly formal floor-length strapless evening gown. After the dessert, the room lights dimmed and a spotlight followed her as she lead the guest speaker to the dais to introduce him. Just before she reached the podium, the guest speaker, who was behind her on the steps and blinded by the spotlight, accidently stepped on the back hem of her dress. She kept going forward. You guessed it: At the moment she turned to face the audience, her strapless gown and everything else was pulled in one swift motion down to the vicinity of her waist. And there she stood, in the spotlight, facing hundreds of people, thinking in a trice: "Lord, if you're going to take me, take me *now*, because I'm never going to make it through this."

Or it can be as devastating as the story—the details of which will be skipped here—related by a Workshop participant about how they felt responsible for the death of their sibling. Again: "Lord, if you're going to take me, take me *now*, because I'm never going to make it through this."

What both of these stories, and so many others like them, have in common is the belief that "This is it! I (my ego) *cannot* survive this. I would pay any price not to have to go through this." We have all been there. More than once. We certainly know how it feels—how desperate, how alone, how foolish, how self-hateful, how stupid, how worthless. And we know how black and suffocating it is. It is a terrible place we feel we will never get through.

Yet, here we are. We may have come through a bit nicked, scarred, and dented. But we made it through, no matter how certain we were we never would. And it has happened more than once. And will most likely happen again.

What does this show us? Two things: 1) The only way out is through—not around or over or under or backing away from; going through it is the only way to get out of it; and 2) We *do* make it through—again and again, because of our strength and resilience.

As you face Risk and Fear, draw strength from what you have already proved to yourself many times. It wasn't luck or fate or anything else that got you through. It was *you*.

And along the way we discover something else, if we take the time and trouble to look past the propaganda of conventional wisdom: Success does nothing more than validate—it says, "You were Right," and that's all—while failure teaches. Little if anything is learned from success. Almost everything we have ever learned we've learned through failure. Do you notice the interesting little paradox this leaves us with: We live in a society that brooks no failure, yet demands that we learn? Go figure . . .

Another expression of the balanced approach—that is, being able to draw from each side of the chart with equal ease—is the Control/Letting Go paradox. When we strive to Control by spending all our time on the *Cosmos* side—following the Rules, gaining Control over others by making them Lose, taking Control by insisting on being Right, by accepting the Order and the Structure to have Safety—we are actually *giving up* Control to all the Structure, Rules, Order, and Winners outside of ourselves. On the other hand, there seems to me to be no greater form of Control than Letting Go. When we are willing to Let Go and not be dependent on other people and/or things to succeed (Win), then we have, in fact, attained the ultimate Control, simply because nothing and/or no one can Control us. *We no longer live according to external whim.* That's what I would call the ultimate Control. And it is another reason why being centered—in perfect balance—between *Cosmos* and *Chaos* is such a powerful position.

And that is why the whole point of this book—and of the Workshop—is for you to reach the perfect balance, your Adult and your Child sharing experiences and, therefore, sharing influence over your reactions to those experiences.

Another part of the balance is between you and others. Sometimes—often, in fact—Play can be enhanced when you include people who want to Play with you. But, as your parents most likely told you several times as you were growing up, "Be careful you don't fall in with the 'Wrong' crowd."

"Great," you say, "but who's the 'Wrong' crowd?" Actually, it's pretty easy to tell. And, of course, Simple. But it's even easier to identify who the "Right" crowd is. We use a particular exercise in the Workshop to make spotting members of the Right crowd both Simple and easy. We do it with toothpicks, 24 of them for each person. And each person lays out their toothpicks like this:

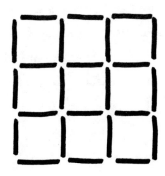

The toothpicks thus laid out constitute a puzzle. The first part of this exercise is to solve the puzzle. And the puzzle is this: Remove eight toothpicks—no more, no less—so that what remains are two equal squares. In the Workshop I take great pains to explain that this exercise is strictly individual and non-verbal. If you're about to solve the puzzle from this book, and there's no one else around, keeping it individual and non-verbal ought to be a snap. Go ahead and give it a shot. Take however much time you need. When you have either solved it, or figure you never will, join me on the next page. I'll wait.

Did you solve it? If you did, you got this:

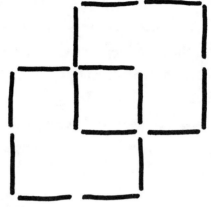

Or you got this:

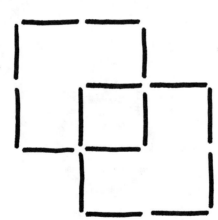

If you didn't get it, perhaps it's because you didn't Hang Out In The Question long enough. You didn't look at it from enough different points of view. After all, I never said the squares couldn't overlap. In any case, you've probably already guessed that solving the puzzle really isn't the point, is it? And you probably already know why: Because the solution of the puzzle is an End, *and this exercise is all about Process.*

The exercise continues. The rest of the instructions those in the Workshop receive before beginning are these: When you have successfully solved the puzzle, stand up (most people do the puzzle sitting on the floor), look around and find someone who is still working on the puzzle, stand next to them, and *assist* them—say nothing, do nothing, except: When the person you are assisting removes a toothpick, and removing that toothpick is part of the solution, applaud. That's it. No talking, no whistling and foot stomping; just applaud. If they remove a toothpick and its removal is *not* part of the solution, do nothing, nothing at all. Be silent and still. When the person you are assisting does solve the puzzle, the two of you find two other people who are still working on it, and go and assist them in the same way.

Eventually, everyone solves the puzzle.

So far, in six years of conducting the Workshop, it always comes down to one person still *trying* to solve the puzzle, and everyone else is crowded around them assisting. That last person almost always spends most of their time staring at the 24 toothpicks —just staring at them—focused on one thing. That thing is (as you have probably already guessed): "I *will* solve this puzzle. I *must* solve this puzzle. I will do it on my own. Anything else is Losing, and I must Win. I must be Right."

The fact is, once one person solves the puzzle, everyone else in the room can solve it *blindfolded* (literally! I've had people do it). How? It is, of course, Simple: Let Go. Let Go of the need to be Right and to Win by solving it on your own. Allow someone to assist. Pick up a toothpick. If your assistant(s) applauds, move it aside. If they do not, put it back. You don't even have to understand the puzzle to solve it. Let Go.

The people who stand next to you and applaud (or not) I call "assistants" for a specific reason. It is because they assist you. They don't help you. The difference may appear subtle, but it is important. When people assist you in doing something, they still allow you to do it. Those who rush in to help you usually end up doing it *for* you. Assistants focus on the Process. Helpers focus on the End. Beware "helpers"—their real purpose may be solely to Win and be Right by making you Lose and be Wrong. After all, you couldn't have done it without them.

Whether you want to use the particular semantic tools I use or not is not important. What is important is that you recognize the difference between the types of aid, and those who offer it.

What else does the exercise demonstrate? It is an excellent model for a support group. A support group assists, it doesn't help (to use my semantics). A support group is honest—not brutal, but honest. A support group doesn't deride you for heading down a dead End during the process, but it does positively support you in keeping the Process going.

A world that insists on Games with Rules can have a crushing, shut-it-down effect on you when you-and-your-Child Want Simply to Play. But that world doesn't have to be a lonely, destructive place. Seek out others who also Want to Play. (You'd be surprised at how many are waiting only to be asked.) You have much in common. Use that common ground as a Playing field, and use this model to create the support group you need to keep the grass on the Playing field green and soft. (And while you're at it, you and your support group can come up with a much better metaphor than that. Let me know what it is.)

There is one last exercise we do in the Workshop. With it, everything that has gone before comes together and is put to use. It is the point where balance is reached. But not until after a bit of struggle.

I call it: The Transformation.

Workshop participants call it: The transformation? And: *The Transformation!* And: *THE TRANSFORMATION?!?* And: **What!?!**

It's a Simple exercise, really. But aren't they all? And, in truth, it's one you, the reader of this book, can do quite independently of the Workshop. Before I tell you how it works, though, it would probably help for you to have just a bit of background about the Workshop context leading up to The Transformation. The Workshop begins on a Friday evening, and it's then I suggest everyone keep their time free Saturday evening. Well, some of it, anyway. It is at

the end of the nine-to-six Saturday Workshop session that I introduce
The Transformation and "hand out assignments." Everyone must
have their Transformation ready by nine Sunday morning. That's all
the background you need.

So here's how it goes:

Do you remember those little Japanese toys that, through
design and manipulation, can "transform" from a rocket ship into a
robot, an airplane into a robot, a car into a robot (they always seemed
to end up as robots—must be a Japanese thing)? Well, that's what
you have to do: Transform from one thing into another (but not
necessarily a robot). In front of everyone else. Right here in this
room. Tomorrow morning.

(That's when hearts beat a little faster and the Room Anxiety
Level (RAL) can be felt going up a notch.)

So you have a better sense of what I'm talking about, here are
some typical Transformations:

- From a "traffic jam" to "the northern lights (aurora
  borealis) shimmering in the night sky."

- From "a vanilla ice cream cone" to "Bette Midler, in concert."

- From "tumbleweed blown about by the wind" to "the volcanic birth of an island."

- From "the immediately-pre-pilgrim Plymouth Rock" to "a thunderstorm followed by a glorious rainbow."

- From "a dress on a hanger" to "Times Square on New Year's Eve, complete with the countdown to midnight."

- From "a pair of binoculars" to "a race car winning a race."

- From "a computer" to "Elvis, in concert."

- From "a falling autumn leaf" to "a grand Fourth of July, complete with fireworks." (How would you do that, considering no incendiary devices are allowed?)

I assign the beginning point of each Transformation, and the ending point. Each person's responsibility is to "be" both of the things of their Transformation to the extent that everyone else present actually experiences them, sees those things before their eyes. And more: The Transformation from beginning to end must be experienced as a gradual (though I never say how gradual) transition, not (as they say in the film business) a hard cut.

("The RAL's goin' up fast, Cap'n. She canna take much more." "Just keep it going, Mr. Scott." "Aye, Cap'n . . .")

You can use—or *not* use—props, wardrobe, makeup, and everything God gave you at birth (like arms, legs, voice). You cannot use any sort of electrical devices. When I call your name, be ready to go.

Pretty simple, huh? How would you do some of those Transformations, considering you'd only have a few hours to come up with it *and* get some sleep?

The Transformation really is a Process, a means of asking everyone to reach further into their Creative power than they probably have for quite some time. Which, of course, also means getting back in touch with *all* the stuff on the *Chaos* side of the chart, and being willing to Let Go, to whatever degree, of their "death grip" (interesting term, huh?) on the stuff on the *Cosmos* side. In other, un-minced words, to get back in balance—the *natural* state.

And it is meant to be a surprise. And an Adventure. They have little time to bury the Process in End-analysis. The Transformation is very much a visual, verbal, vibrant, visceral, (but not necessarily alliterative, like all those v's) sort of thing that brings together Risk and Fear and Play and Adventure. And Creativity. And then urges the shift into Applied Creativity.

In short, it is a Process that moves from an evening of Fear to a morning of (dare I say it?) terror to a climatic and joyous Adult and Child reunion. Or pretty close to that, anyway.

Before the Process of each participant Creating their own unique Transformation (and each one *is* unique) begins (that is, they leave the Workshop for the evening), I go back to the beginning of the Workshop and review where everyone has been, what they have been through, what they have been reminded of and remembered about themselves, and *why* they really are Creatively powerful:

- To unlock your Creative power, you must know where your Creativity is, and you must know everything else you must be willing to unlock to get to it.

- Hang Out In The Question. Resist Answers as long as you can. Build an immense menu of potential and perfectly good Answers to choose from, *then* choose.

- Play. If you aren't Playing, you aren't being Creative. You're only trying to Win, trying to be Safe.

- Risk. Without it there is no Adventure, no discovery.

- There is always another way to look at it.

- You-your-Child is just as valid as you-your-Adult. Listen to that Child earnestly and openly.

- Be honest. Everything else is a waste of time and energy.

- Let Go. It is the ultimate Control. It is freedom from all that would lessen you. Your Creativity—your power—is limited only to the extent you are willing to Let Go.

- Work within your Fear. The Fear will not go away, so you might as well have Fun with it. Remember: 1) The only way out is through; 2) You *do* make it through.

- Acknowledge what it is you Want, and then pursue it passionately.

- You cannot have Win without Lose, you cannot have Right without Wrong. Safety is an illusion.

- No matter what anyone tells you or has told you before, your Child-within-you loves you, and is always eager to Play. Your Child-within-you will *never* refuse your Honest invitation to Play.

- It is you-your-Child who is Creative, not you-your-Adult.

- And always remember the words of the immortal John A. Shedd: "A ship in harbor is Safe, but that is not what ships are built for."

Sunday morning—Transformation morning—is always an astounding display of Creative power. It is honest, and for that reason, it is always perfect. And I am always astonished by the varying perspectives that show up in The Transformations. Such as:

- The woman who was to begin as "a fox which gets caught in a trap," and portrayed a hooker getting busted by an undercover cop.

- The man who was to end as "the Blue Angels climaxing an air show," and portrayed a plane that smashed into the wall, the pilot becoming an angel who was "blue" (sad) that he didn't finish his routine.

There have even been those who showed up Sunday scared to death and not prepared to do anything. They did something anyway: They showed up. They show up full of reasons why they couldn't or Shouldn't or didn't have to do it. ("Lord, if you're going to take me, take me *now*, because I'm never going to make it through this.") So why did they show up? Because by then they had re-experienced enough of the Fun of the *Chaos* side of the chart—something they thought was lost and gone forever—that they didn't Want to give it up. Also, because they were no longer among strangers, but part of a support group they had been a part of Creating.

And with the assistance of that support group, they Let Go of all that Safety and being Right and Winning stuff they had spent the evening with, and did their Transformation right then and there, "off the cuff." And it was perfect. Why? Because it was honest and passionate and spontaneous, and a wonderous demonstration of Creativity. And, most of all, because they Risked just showing up, no matter what their particular "agenda" was. (What a concentrated dose of discovering how powerful their Creativity is. How powerful *they* are. And how balanced. What Fun!)

It works that way because, just like the toothpick puzzle, The Transformation is not about the End, but the Process. How willing are you-your-Adult to share time and space and point of view with you-your-Child? How willing are you to Hang Out In The Question? To look at many different perspectives? To have Fun with Fear? How willing are you to Risk in order to Play and Create? (Don't forget, they all come together in the same package.)

I've had some in the Workshop completely change how they did their Transformations just before—sometimes just moments before

—they began. Because Creativity is a Process. It never stops. Creativity constantly generates perfectly good Answers to choose from without regard to how Right those Answers may be. The more perfectly good Answers to choose from, the merrier you are. Literally.

And it's Fun. Just like a roller coaster. Go ahead, try it. You can do your own Transformation right in the comfort of your own home or office or local gym (depending on how many of whom you're going to do it with/for). You already have all the ingredients, save two. One: Understanding how and/or why I assign the Transformations I do; Two: A transformation assignment. Well, we can take care of those!

- *One*—I assign Transformations in two ways. First, the whole thing must be a challenge—Creatively, and in terms of emotional Risk. Second, I like to assign things which, if anyone cares to take a breather from both the anxiety and Fun of it, they will see illustrates a point about the power of Creativity in their life. Such as: Isn't it nice to be able to get out of the traps all around you ("a fox in a trap"), and soar free to whatever heights you choose ("the Blue Angels")? You have the power to do that. Always have had. Always will.

- *Two*—If you would like to give it a go, contact me through Ramsey Press. Seriously. I'll get back in touch with you as soon as I can, and we'll discuss your own personal Transformation. But only if you really *Want* to.

There is something I say at the end of the Workshop—so I'll also say it here, at the end of this book—which I think is very important. It is this: "You could just as easily call this Workshop 'Unlocking Your Power Creatively' as 'Unlocking Your Creative Power'. They are one and the same."

That's because they come from the same place. When you are at the point of perfect balance on the chart, everything on the *Cosmos* side gives you the practical tools—the pliers—it takes to get where you really Want to go. Everything on the *Chaos* side is the engine that gives you the power to get there.

There is something else I say at the end of the Workshop—and now at the end of this book—of equal importance. It is this: You are the same person now that you were when you began your unlocking Process. *Just more so.* Because now you-your-Adult and you-your-Child are so much more comfortable sharing, experiencing each other's point of view. The two sides of you are back in touch—in perfect balance—and much more willing to honestly Play. And it is *that* which makes you Creative. Always has. Always will.

Go Play.